SALES TRAINING BASICS

REVISED EDITION

Elwood N. Chapman

```
WARNING

FAILURE TO LEARN THESE
SELLING TECHNIQUES
COULD BE HAZARDOUS
TO YOUR WEALTH.
```

CRISP PUBLICATIONS, INC.
Los Altos, California

SALES TRAINING BASICS
A PRIMER FOR THOSE NEW TO SELLING

REVISED EDITION
(Previously published as The Fifty-Minute Sales Training Program)

CREDITS
Editor: **Michael Crisp**
Designer: **Carol Harris**
Typesetting: **Interface Studio**
Cover Design: **Carol Harris**

Copyright © 1986, 1988 by Crisp Publications, Inc.
Printed in the United States of America

Crisp books are distributed in Canada by Reid Publishing, Ltd., P.O. Box 7267, Oakville, Ontario, Canada L6J 6L6.

In Australia by Career Builders, P.O. Box 1051 Springwood, Brisbane, Queensland, Australia 4127.

And in New Zealand by Career Builders, P.O. Box 571, Manurewa, New Zealand.

Library of Congress Catalog Number 85-72733
Chapman, Elwood N.
Sales Training Basics
ISBN O-931961-02-5

PREFACE

Anyone who has customer contact can improve the productivity of his or her organization through the application of the selling techniques in this practical guide. Although ideal to read at the point of employment for those inexperienced in sales, this book is also effective with more experienced employees who wish to review their selling skills.

This book is easy to administer in a program. For individualized instruction, all you need is an employee, a pencil, a chair, and fifty minutes. Because of the low cost, each employee can keep the guide for review and further study. Short seminars or workshops can also be built around the guide.

As you travel through the SALES TRAINING BASICS you will discover a series of lively involvement exercises. These teach the techniques of professional selling, and also stress the importance of a positive attitude. It should go without saying that a positive attitude is a key to the development of effective selling skills.

ABOUT THIS BOOK

SALES TRAINING BASICS is not like most books. It stands out from other self-help books in an important way. It's not a book to read, it's a book to *use.* The unique ''self-paced'' format of this book and the many worksheets, encourage a reader to get involved and, try some new ideas immediately.

This book will provide an awareness and understanding of the basics of selling. Using the simple yet sound techniques presented can help any person new to sales better understand the concepts of what is involved in the selling process.

SALES TRAINING BASICS (and the other books listed on page 55) can be used effectively in a number of ways. Here are some possibilities:

—Self Study. Because the book is self-instructional, all that is needed is a quiet place, and some time. By completing the activities and exercises, a reader should receive practical ideas about how to handle a sales situation regardless of experience.

—Workshops and Seminars. The book is ideal for assigned reading prior to a workshop or seminar. With the basics in hand, the quality of the participation will improve, and more time can be spent on concept extensions and applications. SALES TRAINING BASICS is also effective when it is distributed at the beginning of a session and the participants ''work through'' the contents.

—Remote Location Training. Books can be sent to those not able to attend ''home office'' training sessions.

There are several other possibilities that depend on the objectives, program or ideas of the user.

One thing for sure, even after it has been read, this book will be looked at—and thought about—again and again.

TO THE READER

In approximately fifty minutes you will understand many of the secrets of professional selling. What you learn, and the changes you make after completing this program, are far more important than the time it takes to finish. *Do not read so fast that you miss something.*

Selling should be fun and exciting. You should enjoy it much the same way you do with a favorite sport or pastime. But selling is also a profession with many principles, methods, and skills to be learned. So the best way to become successful at selling is to enjoy it fully, but also learn all you can about the process. It is the combination of a positive attitude and the skills you acquire that will help you become a more productive salesperson.

Good luck!

Elwood N. Chapman

Elwood N. Chapman

P.S. The person who provided this book wants you to enjoy it now, and keep it for future reference. If you have a problem as you proceed, return to this individual for help.

VOLUNTARY
CONTRACT*

I, _____ , hereby agree

(Your Name)

to meet with the individual designated below within

thirty days to discuss my progress toward incorporating the

techniques and ideas presented in this program. The purpose

of this meeting will be to *review* areas of strength and

establish action steps for areas where improvement may

still be required.

_____

Signature

I agree to meet with the above individual on

_____

Month   *Date*   *Time*

at the following location.

_____

_____

Signature

*This agreement can be initiated either by you or your superior.
Its purpose is to motivate you to incorporate concepts and
techniques of this program into your daily activities, and
provide a degree of accountability.

CONTENTS

ATTITUDE PLUS BASIC SELLING SKILLS EQUALS SUCCESS

Attitude is so important to employers that they often will hire an employee because of a positive attitude more than the level of that person's education, or previous selling experience. This happens because a positive attitude (unlike selling skills) is almost impossible to teach. Because of this, the short message below has a special meaning.

We are not always conscious that we <u>show</u> our mental attitudes to others. To help you become more aware of attitude, the drawings in this book have been designed to resemble the tiny amoeba which is often referred to as a beginning form or life. All of the amoeba drawings reflect common attitudes.

"After all, I'm just an amoeba."

Their purpose in this publication is to remind you how important a positive attitude is in all selling and customer contact situations. Whether you meet a prospective customer for the first time, encounter a customer relations problem, or practice the skills you will learn in this guide, it is always good to remember YOUR ATTITUDE IS SHOWING! Perhaps the tiny amoeba will help remind you how important your attitude is.

E. N. Chapman

MAKE YOUR CHOICE NOW

SUCCESSES

FAILURES

Those who learn and then practice accepted sales techniques.

Those who remain positive.

Salespeople who listen to their prospects.

Individuals who know the products they sell.

Salespeople who learn to manage their time and set priorities.

Those who consider themselves problem solvers.

Add your own:

_____

_____

_____

_____

Those who depend 100% upon their personalties.

Individuals who turn negative.

Those who do all the talking and never learn a customer's needs.

Salespeople who don't bother learning product features and benefits.

Individuals who are more interested in their commissions than their prospects.

Salespeople who refuse to learn from their mistakes.

Add your own:

_____

_____

_____

_____

The difference between an effective and ineffective salesperson is usually a matter of sensitivity, sincerity, attitude, and selling skills—all of which can be learned.

Case studies help provide insights you may not already possess. Five case problems are included in this program. Please give them your careful attention.

The case on the opposite page will help you understand the personal value of sales training.

Personality obviously plays an important role in the selling process. This is why some people claim that successful salespeople are born and not made. But is personality all that is necessary? Aren't there skills that true professional salespeople use? The answer is yes. Professionals use a wide variety of techniques to approach clients, present products, answer questions, and close sales. Each selling situation requires that these techniques be adapted and skillfully used, * but the basics that everyone needs to learn remain the same.

CASE 1

* For an excellent book aimed at Professional Salespeople write CRISP PUBLICATIONS for information on a new book, by Rebecca Morgan.

A DECISION FOR RAMONA

Ramona, now 27 with two children, has decided to enter the labor market. Although she has a friendly nature and dresses with style, Ramona lacks self-confidence and has trouble initiating conversation in social situations. Yesterday Ramona was offered a sales training opportunity in a high-fashion department store. When she talked to her husband about the offer, he downplayed the job. ''I think you are attracted to the glamour of working with fancy clothes and not considering how difficult it is to deal with demanding customers. You had good clerical skills at one time, why not brush up on them and look for an office job?''

The following morning Ramona talked the job offer over with her good friend Marci. After hearing Ramona's description, Marci was enthusiastic about the opportunity. ''It seems ideal to me, Ramona. You have never been in a situation where you have to meet new people and this job will help you learn to be more outgoing. The job is kind of a personality development school where you will learn to deal effectively with all kinds of people. Since you know clothes, it should be easy. In my view being trained as a professional salesperson will benefit you in your future career choices. The person who offered you the job must see your potential. Go for it!''

    I agree with Ramona's husband.
    I agree with Marci.

Please turn to page 54 and compare your thoughts to those of the author.

IF YOU HAVE CUSTOMER CONTACT, YOU HAVE SELLING OPPORTUNITIES

When you think of professional selling positions in retail stores, insurance and real estate firms, or in direct home selling (Avon calling!) you expect these individuals have received formal sales training. But what about bank tellers, receptionists, supermarket checkers, food servers, hotel clerks, flight attendants, or telephone service representatives? Could they also benefit themselves and their organizations with sales training?

The answer is an unqualified yes. Most employees, whether they recognize it or not, engage to some degree in the selling process. For example, bank tellers and loan officers may not sell tangibles but they have a list of important services to offer customers. Anyone dealing with the public is engaged in customer relations which sells customers on returning to that organization whenever a product or service is needed.

Many of the basic selling techniques used by professional sales people are useful by anyone who has customer contact.

WHAT CAN SUCCESS IN SELLING DO FOR YOU?

In addition to a higher income; learning professional selling techniques can do many *personal* things for you. *Three* of the ten statements below are false. Place a check in the square opposite the false statements, and match your answers with those at the bottom of the page.

☐ 1. Dealing with customers is more exciting than the routine work involved in most other jobs.

☐ 2. Selling brings out the best in your personality.

☐ 3. Salespeople are made, not born; if you don't plan and work hard, you'll never be exceptional at selling.

☐ 4. Few executives start out as salespeople.

☐ 5. Those good at selling can often quickly improve their income.

☐ 6. Learning to sell now will help you succeed in *any* job in the future.

☐ 7. In your first sales job, what you learn can be more important than what you earn.

☐ 8. Selling is less demanding than other jobs.

☐ 9. You have less freedom in most selling positions.

☐ 10. A smile uses fewer muscles than a frown.

FALSE STATEMENTS.

4. Many claim early selling experiences helped them become executives.

8. Selling is more demanding because you must stay positive all the time.

9. Most selling jobs—especially those outside—provide far more freedom than more confining positions.

View your first selling position as an opportunity to test your personality potential.

YOUR ATTITUDE IS SHOWING

WHAT IS A POSITIVE ATTITUDE?

On the surface, attitude is the way you communicate your mood or disposition to customers or co-workers. When you are optimistic and anticipate successful encounters with others, you transmit a positive attitude and they usually respond favorably. When you are pessimistic and expect the worst, your attitude often is negative and customers will tend to avoid you. Inside your head, where it all starts, attitude is a mind set. IT IS THE WAY YOU LOOK AT THINGS MENTALLY.

YOUR ATTITUDE TOWARD SELLING

To be an effective salesperson—you must first have a positive attitude. Nothing else has a higher priority. A positive attitude is the way you look at things—in this case selling. To measure your attitude toward selling, complete this exercise. If you circle a 5, you are saying your attitude could not be better in this area; if you circle a 1, you are saying selling is probably not for you.

	Agree				Disagree
There is nothing demeaning about selling a product or service to a prospect.	5	4	3	2	1
I would be proud to tell friends selling is my career.	5	4	3	2	1
I can approach customers, regardless of age, appearance, or behavior, with a positive attitude.	5	4	3	2	1
On bad days—when nothing goes right—I can still be positive.	5	4	3	2	1
I am enthusiastic about selling.	5	4	3	2	1
Having customers turn me down will not cause me to be negative.	5	4	3	2	1
The idea of selling challenges me.	5	4	3	2	1
Selling is a profession.	5	4	3	2	1
Good salespeople are problem-solvers.	5	4	3	2	1
Selling is a great way to make a living.	5	4	3	2	1

TOTAL

If you scored above 40, you have an excellent attitude toward selling as a profession. If you rated yourself between 25 and 40, you appear to have serious reservations. A rating under 25 indicates another type of job would probably be best for you.

YOU DO NOT NEED
TO BE AN
EXTROVERT TO
BE
SUCCESSFUL AT SELLING.

QUIET,
THOUGHTFUL PEOPLE OFTEN
ARE VERY
SUCCESSFUL.

IT TAKES PERSONAL CONFIDENCE
TO BE GOOD AT SELLING

SELF-CONFIDENCE SCALE

You may have rated high in attitude, but if you do not have the confidence to meet customers, all is lost. This exercise is designed to help you measure your self-confidence. Read the statements and then circle the number you feel best fits you.

	High				Low
I can convert strangers into friends quickly and easily.	5	4	3	2	1
I can attract and hold the attention of others even when I do not know them.	5	4	3	2	1
I love new situations.	5	4	3	2	1
I'm intrigued with the psychology of meeting and building a good relationship with someone I do not know.	5	4	3	2	1
I would enjoy making a sales presentation to a group of executives.	5	4	3	2	1
When dressed for the occasion, I have great confidence in myself.	5	4	3	2	1
I do not mind using the telephone to make appointments with strangers.	5	4	3	2	1
Others do not intimidate me.	5	4	3	2	1
I enjoy solving problems.	5	4	3	2	1
Most of the time, I feel secure.	5	4	3	2	1

TOTAL

If you scored high on both the attitude and self-confidence exercises, you have a winning combination as far as selling is concerned. If you scored lower on self-confidence than attitude, you are receiving a signal that you need more experience dealing with people. This program can help increase your self-confidence.

CHARACTERISTICS OF SUCCESSFUL SALESPEOPLE

Sometimes quiet, unassuming salespeople become highly successful because they are accepted more easily by customers who resent those more aggressive. At other times salespeople who are more outgoing and verbal are successful because they communicate an immediate warmth that dissipates the psychological barriers some customers have toward being sold something. That is why there are so many different successful models in the field of professional selling. The only characteristic that everyone needs to succeed is a postitive attitude.

Following are ten common personality characteristics found in successful salespeople. Place a plus in the square opposite those traits you already possess, a check mark opposite those you can more fully develop in the future, and a question mark in any remaining squares.

- ☐ Self-starter
- ☐ Persistent
- ☐ Like people
- ☐ Energetic
- ☐ Problem solver
- ☐ Good communicator
- ☐ Not easily frustrated
- ☐ Ambitious
- ☐ Like money
- ☐ Enjoy recognition
- ☐ Friendly

CASE 2

WILL JOE SURVIVE?

Study this situation carefully and decide whether you feel Joe will succeed as a professional salesperson.

Fresh out of college, Joe accepted a high-paying but demanding sales position with enthusiasm. A physical education major, Joe planned to be a high school football coach but could not find a suitable coaching position in the geographical area of his choice; so he turned to sales.

Big, handsome and something of a free spirit, Joe has no fear of people or situations. He speaks up quickly, has considerable self-confidence and is meticulous about his appearance. With his energy and personality, Joe is easy to like. Best of all, Joe does not give up easily. His athletic training taught him that you never give up until the game is over. On top of all this, Joe has natural leadership ability. In his senior year he was, among other things, captain of the defensive football team.

During his two-week, sales training, it became obvious that Joe did not always take selling techniques seriously. Somehow, he felt he didn't need to learn how to play the game because his personality would see him through. In group training sessions, and when he was assigned to a professional salesperson to gain experience with live prospects, Joe appeared to be listening. Later, however, when he had an opportunity to demonstrate what he had learned, he relied on his own ideas. In those instances, when Joe was permitted to approach a prospect on his own, he did most of the talking and did not make a serious attempt to understand the prospect's point of view. Despite his poor listening skills, everyone in the firm (especially fellow sales trainees) likes Joe, and many feel he is a natural salesperson. Most predict early success for Joe.

What is your opinion? Will Joe succeed and become a long-term professional? Check the appropriate box below, and compare your decision with that of the author on page 54.

☐ Joe will succeed.

☐ Joe will eventually fail.

FIRST IMPRESSIONS ARE CRITICAL

Because customers have different values and personal standards, some employers encourage their salespeople to communicate a safe or conservative image. Employers in some environments (restaurants) require uniforms; others (sophisticated fashion stores) ask their salespeople to adhere to dress codes. When accepting a new position, it is a good idea to discuss the matter of grooming and image before reporting to work.

COMMUNICATING YOUR BEST IMAGE

Like an actor or actress, a person who has customer contact is always on stage. Creating a good first impression is essential. It is, also, important to understand that there is a direct connection between how you look to yourself and your self-confidence. The better your self-image, the more positive your attitude will be. Please rate yourself on each of the grooming areas presented below. If you circle a 5, you are saying that no improvement is required. If you circle a 1 or 2, you need considerable improvement. Be honest.

	Perfect	*Good*	*Fair*	*Weak*	*Poor*
Hairstyle, hair and/or beard grooming.	5	4	3	2	1
Personal habits of cleanliness.	5	4	3	2	1
Selection of clothing (appropriate to the situation).	5	4	3	2	1
Clothing color coordination.	5	4	3	2	1
Neatness (shoes shined, clothes clean, well-pressed, etc.).	5	4	3	2	1
General grooming: Do you feel your appearance will reflect professionalism?	5	4	3	2	1

When it comes to appearance, I would rate myself:

☐ Excellent   ☐ Good   ☐ Need Improvement

> **Most successful salespeople claim that to be sharp mentally you must communicate your best image.**

SELLING STYLE

Each person new to a selling situation must adapt his or her style to the environment. It is one thing to sell complicated computer systems to a foreign prospect; something quite different to sell cosmetics to a teenager. Listen to your supervisor. Observe co-workers. Then develop a selling style which best fits your customers, products and services. As you do this, keep in mind that the techniques presented in this book fit comfortably into any style. Also there some few fundamentals that apply universally. You will discover some of these on the facing page.

TOOLS OF THE TRADE

THE PSYCHOLOGY OF SELLING

Here are some tips (psychological tools of the trade) that should help you demonstrate you are on your way to becoming an effective salesperson.

Make customers feel good about themselves. When you listen respectfully, help clients make a decision and then compliment them for making a good one, you help them feel better about themselves. This creates a better relationship between you and your customer.

Expect to be turned down now and then. The sports phrase ''you can't win them all'' is helpful in selling. Program yourself for some disappointments so you won't dwell on defeat when it occurs.

Acknowledge you don't have all the answers to a complex problem. A professional consultant (and smart salesperson) contributes to a solution by working with the client as a partner, not as a know-it-all.

Turn disappointment into an advantage. When you have a good relationship with a client, even if you don't get the sale, it is possible to open the door to future opportunities. For example, the client may refer you to another prospect or, as often happens, buy from you at a future date.

A bird in the hand is worth ten in the bush. Do not be naive about your selling expectations. A sale has not been made until the money is in the bank. Too many times a new salesperson assumes an order without making certain it is secure.

Organize your time. Most salespeople who experience difficulties do so because they do not prepare a daily plan of action. A disorganized salesperson winds up frustrated, discouraged and with few orders. An organized salesperson enjoys a feeling of accomplishment.

SELLING
IS
LIKE
PLAYING
BASEBALL

SELLING AS A GAME

Professional salespeople like to consider selling as a game for many reasons. You hear them saying: "Everyday is a new ballgame." "Sometimes you do everything right and still strike out."

The truth is that playing a "game" is more motivating than "work" and selling lends itself to the game concept.

COVER ALL THE BASES AND MAKE A SALE

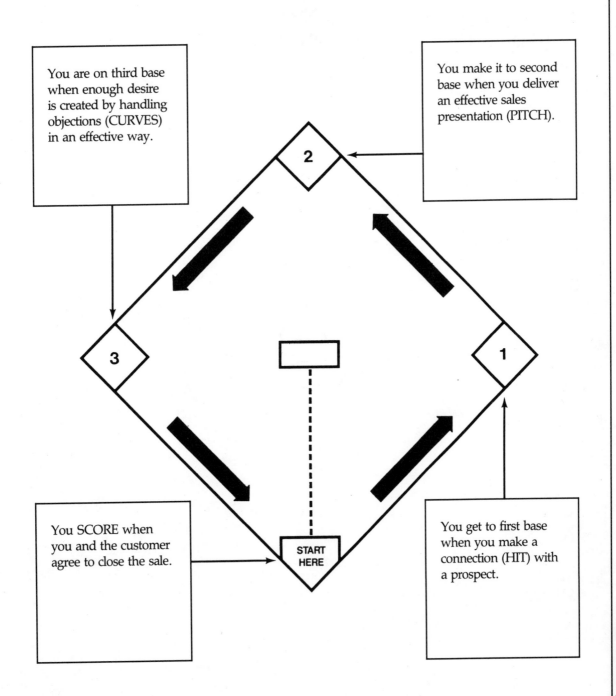

You are on third base when enough desire is created by handling objections (CURVES) in an effective way.

You make it to second base when you deliver an effective sales presentation (PITCH).

2

3

1

START HERE

You SCORE when you and the customer agree to close the sale.

You get to first base when you make a connection (HIT) with a prospect.

TIPS ON HOW TO
GET TO FIRST BASE:
MAKE YOUR APPROACH TO THE
PROSPECT PROFESSIONAL,
PERCEPTIVE, AND POSITIVE.

MOST BATTERS DO NOT GET TO FIRST BASE

If you don't get to first base with a prospective customer, the game is over before it begins. Here are four tips that will help you get off on the right foot with customers.

Send friendly non-verbal signals. A warm smile, solid eye contact, good posture, grooming, and the way you walk are all examples of non-verbal signals. Most important of all is your attitude. When greeting a prospect make sure your non-verbal signals are appropriate before you say anything. Project confidence.

Use a verbal greeting that is sincere, warm, and natural. What you say and how you say it will help both you and your prospect relax. Conversation of a light nature will help break the ice with your prospect.

Demonstrate an immediate desire to help. Act more like a consultant or advisor than a person selling something. This may mean asking questions and listening carefully to what your prospect says. The better the communications now, the easier it will be for you to get to second base later.

Discover customer needs. Unless you discover the needs of a prospect, you can't satisfy them. The effective use of questions will allow prospects to share their problems. If you can help solve the problem, you will probably make the sale. If you can't honestly satisfy any need or solve the problem, say so. Your time, and that of the prospect, is valuable; and your honesty will be respected.

> **Note: It is important to qualify a potential customer early. A true prospect is someone who has the need for what you sell, the authority to buy it, and the money to pay for it. It is foolish for you to run around the bases only to be put out at home because you didn't qualify the prospect in the first place.**

GET TO SECOND BASE BY MAKING A *PROFESSIONAL* PRESENTATION:

KNOW WHAT YOU ARE SELLING

The more you know about the product and/or service your organization provides, the more help you can be to a customer. Those who sell one line of products (computers, stocks and bonds, automobile) have the advantage of focus. They have the luxury of becoming experts at what they sell.

This concentration is not always possible in other areas. Here are two examples.

(1) Salespeople in retail stores have a wide variety of ever-changing products to sell. Because of this they often must depend upon product labels, co-workers, or even customers for product knowledge.

(2) Banks and Savings and Loan institutions often have dozens of different services for their customers. A branch manager or loan officer often has trouble staying up to date, let alone a teller who must deal first with routine customer transactions. As a result, tellers must learn to understand how to make pleasant transfers to more knowledgable parties.

SECOND BASE IS NOT AUTOMATIC

After you are on first base, the prospect should be ready to listen to your sales story. You will, for a time, be in command. Make the most of the opportunity you have earned by following the tips below.

Find the hot button: Different prospects buy the same product or service for different reasons (status, performance, cost, etc.). If you listen carefully, they will tell you what appeals to them. When you discover this "hot button" you should be able to steer your presentation more in that direction.

Use visuals: You can communicate better and hold the interest of the prospect longer if you can show as well as tell. If you do not have any formal visuals, a pencil and pad can be effective. You will appear more professional when you do this.

Ask for feedback: It is vital to know if the prospect is listening. Now and then ask questions like—'Does that make sense?' and 'Will that help solve your problem?' To make progress, you must know what the prospect is thinking.

Tell a complete story: If you forget to tell a prospect a key feature about your product or service, you may miss the sale. On the other hand, you don't want to give the prospect more information than is required or desired.

RULE OF THREE

In many retail selling situations, you have the opportunity to present different alternatives of the same product. This is true when selling shoes, clothing, tools, etc. In presenting these kinds of products, show only three varieties at any one time. If you wish to introduce a fourth product, eliminate one already shown. Research has shown that customers do well deciding among three products; however, with more than three confusion sets in. This technique will allow you to begin to close the sale by asking: "Which would you prefer?"

FACTS VS BENEFITS

We all know that an advantage of a polyester shirt is that you can wash it at night and wear it the next morning. No ironing is necessary. In selling such a shirt, polyester is the fact. The benefit is that it saves the customer time and money by drying quickly without wrinkling.

Most customers are more interested in benefits than facts. Talk benefits but keep in mind that the more you know about the products or services the better prepared you will be to answer questions. It is always a good idea to know more about a product than you normally use in a presentation.

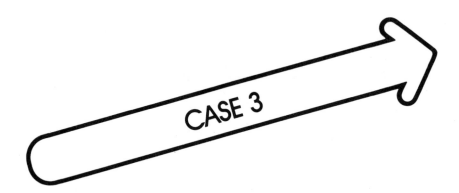

CASE 3

WHO MADE THE SALE?

Although they work for competitive firms, Mary and Sally are equally competent as decorators and each has good sales skills. A few weeks ago both were invited to make a sales presentation to a church committee assigned the task of installing new carpeting in the sanctuary. Over $10,000.00 is budgeted for this job.

Mary takes pride knowing all of her products, especially carpeting. She reads all available printed materials in addition to asking questions of suppliers. She has visited carpeting mills so she fully understands carpeting construction. During her presentation, Mary stressed the wear factor in the two carpets she recommended, discussed safety factors for senior members, and went into detail on the ease of maintenance. She was prepared to answer any and all questions relative to the advantages and benefits of her carpeting over others on the market. Many questions were asked.

Sally has been content to learn only what she really needs to know about any product she sells. Her concentration is on the psychological benefits of the product on the consumer. She pushes brand names but avoids specifics about the product. In her presentation, she stressed the improved religious atmosphere the carpet would create and the impact the beautiful color would have on church members. Sally is entertaining as well as persuasive in making presentations.

Assume that both Mary and Sally wind up recommending the exact carpet— same color, same price, same installation arrangements. Who, in your opinion, would make the sale? Place a check in the box of your choice below, and then turn to page 54 to compare your answer with that of the author.

☐ Mary would make the sale.   ☐ Sally would make the sale.

MAKE THE MOVE
TO THIRD BASE

AVOID ASKING PREMATURE QUESTIONS

Once you have qualified a prospect by asking investigative questions in a nice way, it is usually best to wait for additional questions or objections to come from the customer. The primary reason for this is that questions from a prospect are easier to deal with. For example, if you ask a customer how much she/he is prepared to pay for your product, you may eliminate it from consideration before you have had a chance to communicate its value. If you ask what color coat your prospect is interested in, you might have trouble finding the color requested. Why not give yourself the advantage by waiting for such questions to come from the customer naturally?

WELCOME QUESTIONS
(LET THE CUSTOMER TAKE YOU TO THIRD BASE)

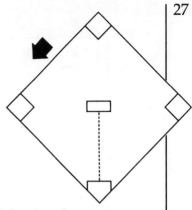

Most customers decide to buy by asking questions. How you answer these questions will determine whether you get to third base or become stranded on second. Here are four suggestions.

Encourage and welcome all questions. The moment you become defensive about your product or service is the moment you lose the game. Listen carefully to each question (or objection) before you start to answer it.

Honest answers, please. Customers will not buy if they have doubts about the quality of a product. If your product has a disadvantage, first acknowledge it and then compensate by pointing out an advantage that outweighs the disadvantage. A product or a service need not be perfect for the prospect to buy. It only needs to be a solution for the customer.

Explain why new is better than old. Here you become more of a teacher than a salesperson. Make comparisons; demonstrate why performance will improve; show how the prospect will come out ahead with your product.

Introduce the Mutual Reward Theory. Explain that in any sound sales transaction, both parties should benefit. Remind prospects that you could not expect any future purchases from them unless they come out ahead now. When the prospect realizes you are sincere, you will finally be on third base.

SELLING IS A PROBLEM-SOLVING PROCESS

Customers buy products and services to solve their problems or enhance their position. Always try to view the problem (or opportunity) as the prospect sees it. Acting as a consultant instead of a salesperson will put you in a position to communicate better, because your insights will provide reasons your product or service can help solve the problem.

PLAY TO WIN

By the time you and the prospect get to third base, you have probably invested considerable time and energy. All this is lost if you don't score (i.e. land the sale). There is something very fulfilling when you win. Winning may not be everything as some coaches say (in selling you want a satisfied customer), but it is the primary reward of any professional salesperson.

CLOSING THE SALE

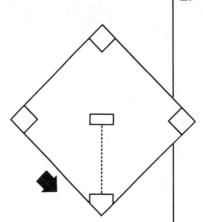

Many baseball teams could have made it to the World Series if they had not stranded so many base runners. Many failures in selling could have been avoided if the salesperson learned how to close a sale. Have confidence in the progress you made getting to third base, but make sure you get home by following with these actions.

Summarize advantages. Frequently, at the end of the selling process, the prospect needs to see all the advantages in one, clear, concise package. This summary makes a ''yes'' decision much easier.

Introduce financial arrangements. You can close a sale by finalizing financial arrangements. When the customer agrees to a financial plan, the sale is usually consummated.

Use a powerful closing statement. Sometimes a single sentence will get you home safely. For example, you might say: ''It appears you have found the best solution to your problem. Why delay?''

Ask for the order. Do it in your own way, but under no conditions should you hesitate to ask the prospect to buy. The fact that you covered the first three bases gives you the right to make a play for home plate. If you need additional confidence, consider that getting stranded on third may hurt the prospect as much, or more, than it will hurt you.

HOW *MUCH* PERSUASION?

- Some prospects will back away if they feel pressured

- Some prospects will not buy unless they are sold

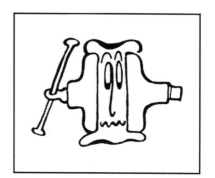

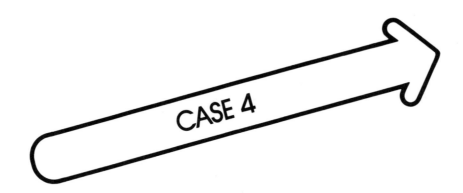

WHO CLOSED THE SALE?

Please assume in dealing with this case that the following three factors exist:

Factor 1 Both Sara and Marlow are equally successful salespeople with similar experience. Both work on a commission basis and the sale in question would mean not only a substantial amount of income but would, also, go a long way in helping them reach their quota.

Factor 2 Although they work for different firms, they are selling basically the same product at the same price. Other conditions are similar.

Factor 3 Sara and Marlow have done equally well getting the same prospect to third base. The winner will be the person who does the best job closing the sale.

In her closing, Sara summarized what she said to get the prospect to third base. She stressed the reliability of her product and the reputation of her company. She insured her prospect understood that the product will be delivered on schedule. Sara committed herself to train those involved in the use of the product after it was installed. Sara's closing sentence to the prospect was: "If you give me the order, you won't be disappointed."

Marlow, in his attempt to close the sale, used a different approach. He zeroed in on the problem of the prospect. He indicated that the prospect's organization would continue to lose money until a solution had been reached. His voice slowly increased in volume as he built to a climax designed to win him an immediate "yes." Marlow's closing sentence was: "I'm convinced you have found the best answer to your problem with my product. May I have your order?"

Who, in your opinion, would have closed the sale? Place a check in the box of your choice below and then turn to page 54 to compare your answer with that of the author.

☐ Sara closed the sale.   ☐ Marlow closed the sale.

☐ Both Sara and Marlow closed the sale.

BEFORE YOU CONTINUE, TAKE A MINUTE TO MAKE SURE YOU HAVE THE BASIC STEPS OF SELLING DOWN PAT.

REVIEW

PROVE YOU ARE READY TO SELL

In the weeks ahead, keep the comparison between baseball and selling in your mind. Make a serious attempt to fully cover all four bases in each transaction. To help you do this, please write out (in your own words) the missing technique for each base. Once you have done your best, return to the pages indicated to match your answers.

<table>
<tr>
<td>

THIRD BASE techniques
(Page 27)

1. Encourage questions and objections.
2. Honest answers, please.
3. _____
   _____
4. Introduce the Mutual Reward Theory.

</td>
<td>

SECOND BASE techniques
(Page 23)

1. Locate and press the hot button.
2. _____
   _____
3. Ask for feedback.
4. Tell the complete story.

</td>
</tr>
<tr>
<td>

GETTING HOME techniques
(Page 29)

1. Summarize advantages.
2. Introduce financial arrangements.
3. Use a powerful closing sentence.
4. _____
   _____

</td>
<td>

FIRST BASE techniques
(Page 21)

1. Send friendly non-verbal signals.
2. Use a verbal greeting that is sincere, warm, and natural.
3. Demonstrate a desire to help.
4. _____
   _____

</td>
</tr>
</table>

REMAINING POSITIVE
IS THE GREATEST
CHALLENGE OF
SELLING.

Selling environments often present "up" and "down" attitude situations. For example, it is usually easy to remain positive during peak hours, days, or seasons when the environment is alive and active. It is more difficult when things are inactive. On top of this, when things are active, customers seem easier to satisfy. During slow periods they seem to demand more. Even bosses and supervisors are more difficult when business activity is low. All of this makes it extremely difficult for any salesperson to maintain a positive attitude over an extended period of time. Some experts claim it is the number one challenge!

ELIMINATING DOWN PERIODS

In life, it is impossible to be ''up'' all the time. Everyone including the most successful salespeople, have down days. This exercise assumes three things: (1) You are generally a positive person. (2) There are certain things you can do to remain positive. (3) Becoming aware of them can assist you to remain positive.

The action steps listed below help some people maintain their positive attitudes. After reading the list, select the three you feel will do the most for you.

☐ Engage in physical exercise of some sort.

☐ Give yourself more attainable goals.

☐ Try to take life less seriously.

☐ Share your positive attitude with others.

☐ Take more week-end or ''mini'' vacations.

☐ Maintain a better balance between work and leisure.

☐ Emphasize your grooming more.

☐ Devote more time seeking inner harmony (go to church, do yoga, or read a good book, etc.).

☐ Do more for others.

☐ Seek out those who can provide positive reinforcement for you.

Others: _____

_____

_____

SUCCESSFUL IDEAS AHEAD

RELATED SELLING

In many selling situations (such as retailing), once a customer decides to buy she/he becomes a good prospect for additional sales.

Some products go together.

Paint, brush, thinner, drop cloth, etc.

Coat, shirt, tie, etc.

Lipstick, eye shadow, powder, etc.

Hamburger, french fries.

Personal computer, software, printer, supplies, etc.

In these situations, the salesperson does the customer a favor by suggesting related items which might save an extra shopping trip or make the original purchase more usable.

BECOME AN EXPERT AT RELATED SELLING!

LITTLE THINGS COUNT

Read the following ideas. Place a check in those boxes where you agree with the statement.

☐ 1. Once a sales has been consummated, it is best to thank the customer and move along to your next activity.

☐ 2. It is more difficult to replace a customer than to keep one satisfied.

☐ 3. Never make a promise to a customer unless you and your organization will be able to keep it.

☐ 4. Always endeavor to radiate confidence in yourself and in your products and/or services.

☐ 5. An excellent way to handle a disappointment is to forget it and go right back to work.

☐ 6. A salesperson should not criticize or condemn competitors.

☐ 7. A salesperson should show respect for the opinions of a customer.

☐ 8. It is usually a good idea to let customers feel that an idea you introduced belongs to them.

☐ 9. Even when customers are wrong, they should be treated with sensitivity.

☐ 10. Nothing can take the place of a smile.

☐ 11. The moment that selling becomes work (instead of a game) a person becomes less effective.

☐ 12. Often your attitude speaks more loudly to customers than anything you say.

**EMPLOYERS ARE ALWAYS LOOKING FOR
QUALIFIED SALESPEOPLE**

SELLING VIA THE TELEPHONE

In the future, more and more selling will be done via the telephone. This is called telemarketing. The reason it will occur is because making personal sales calls is becoming increasingly expensive.

This suggests that whenever possible you should use the telephone and use it effectively.

EXAMPLES

PROFESSIONAL SALESPEOPLE HAVE ALWAYS USED THE TELEPHONE TO KEEP IN TOUCH WITH KEY CUSTOMERS.

TELEPHONE OPPORTUNITIES
(Let your fingers make you successful)

| Hazel | Hazel is the number one salesperson in the appliance department. When she is not on the floor with a customer you will find her on the telephone talking to prospects or keeping in touch with previous customers. For example, she makes a practice of contacting customers who have just made a purchase to make sure the installation was made on time and that everything is working right. Other salespeople in her department do not bother to do this. Hazel made this statement when presented with an award recently: ''I'm not a better salesperson than the others, I just use the telephone as a partner or second salesperson to build better relationships.'' |

| Ramon | Ramon is an outside salesperson representing a sporting goods wholesaler. His territory is the entire state of Arizona. Last year, to cut down on travel expenses, Ramon got permission from his customers to call on them every four months instead of every two. To compensate, he promised to telephone them once each month to take orders, make suggestions, and handle problems. As a result, Ramon has increased sales 20%, cut travel expenses 40%, and now spends more time at home with his family. To the amazement of his sales manager, customers seemed as satisfied as previously. |

| Genelle | Genelle sells a line of cosmetics to drug chains and large department stores. She is most effective with sophisticated cosmetic buyers and on scheduled days does make-up demonstrations for customers. Genelle's only problem is that taking care of key accounts gives her little time to contact smaller drug stores, family department stores, and other retailers who could profit from her line. As a result of careful analysis, Genelle discovered that her most ineffective day in working the key accounts was Monday. On an experimental basis, she decided to stay home each Monday and, use the telephone to contact smaller accounts. In doing this, she worked out a telephone presentation that allowed her to cover all four bases. Also, she would always thank the prospect for permitting her to make a telephone instead of a personal contact. After perfecting her telephone presentation, Genelle was able to increase sales by 15% without neglecting any key accounts. |

HOW TO BE A
TELEPHONE PROFESSIONAL

(It's not as easy as you think)

Two major factors are involved in successful telephone marketing or selling. First, you are dependent upon the tone and quality of your voice to communicate a positive, friendly attitude that will get you to first base. Second, your introductory remarks are critical because you do not have the advantage of eye contact and smiling with potential customers.

Most experts recommend you introduce yourself by name, state the organization you represent, and if possible, use the name of a third party to get you started. The idea is to create interest and intrigue about yourself and the purpose of your call.

To improve your telephone approach, you might consider experimenting on a home message recorder (your own or one belonging to a friend). Prepare your introductory remarks ahead of time, make the call and deliver your message. Then listen to your message and react to your voice as though you were the potential customer.

DOING A NUMBER
ON THE TELEPHONE

Successful salespeople make better use of the telephone than almost any other profession. The following exercise should measurably improve your telephone techniques by helping you discover what you may be doing wrong. Circle the appropriate response. Further instructions are provided at the bottom of the page.

HOW OFTEN DO YOU:	NEVER	SELDOM	SOME-TIMES	OFTEN	ALWAYS	IMPROVE-MENT NEEDED
Think about calling a prospect but fail to do so.	1	2	3	4	5	☐
Put a smile into your voice as you pick up the receiver.	5	4	3	2	1	☐
Fail to return a client call.	1	2	3	4	5	☐
Communicate a positive attitude.	5	4	3	2	1	☐
Sound annoyed when you answer a call.	1	2	3	4	5	☐
Solicit customer feedback by telephone.	1	2	3	4	5	☐
Accomplish the same results by phone as you would from a personal call.	5	4	3	2	1	☐
Save travel time through effective use of the telephone.	1	2	3	4	5	☐
Cover all four bases by telephone in a professional manner.	5	4	3	2	1	☐
End the conversation with a pleasant, upbeat comment after summarizing the reasons for the call.	5	4	3	2	1	☐

If you circled a 3, 4, or 5, your selling telephone techniques need improvement, check those squares in the right hand column where you are serious about making improvements.

YOU'LL BECOME MORE PROFESSIONAL IF YOUR MANAGER ESTABLISHES HIGH STANDARDS AND HELPS YOU TO REACH THEM THROUGH TRAINING AND ENCOURAGEMENT.

Most sales supervisors or managers started out knowing little about the selling process. They reached their present positions because they developed and applied many skills. As a result, they know that you, too, can be successful selling. In some cases they will insist that you learn and apply skills that *they* have found successful. In other cases, they will leave you develop your *own* style. The fact that these managers have high expectations for you is good. If you welcome this attitude on their part you will become a professional salesperson sooner.

SELF-MOTIVATING IDEAS

REWARD YOURSELF

Getting a hit, stealing a base, and scoring a run in a baseball game are rewarding. In selling, the ultimate reward is making the sale. Those who are successful in doing this often motivate themselves with a series of personal rewards they create ahead of time. Below are some rewards you might find motivating. Keep in mind that such rewards should be enjoyed *after* you accomplish some of your goals.

Daily Rewards
{
Going to a health spa at the end of the day.

Dining at a favorite restaurant.

Spending time with a special person.

Other:_____

_____

Weekly Rewards
{
Going for a week-end trip.

Attending a concert or sporting event.

Other:_____

_____

Monthly Rewards
{
Taking a ''mini-vacation''.

Making a special purchase.

Other:_____

_____

Annual Rewards
{
Achieving special recognition for your sales performance.

Taking a special trip such as foreign travel.

Other:_____

_____

THE DIFFICULT CUSTOMER

Listed below are ten ways to react to an over-demanding or otherwise hostile customer. ONLY FOUR ARE ACCEPTABLE FORMS OF BEHAVIOR. Place a check in the box opposite those you believe to be acceptable and match your opinions with those at the bottom of the page.

☐ 1. Show slight disgust on your face so the customer will know you consider him or her a problem.

☐ 2. Challenge the customer with your eyes.

☐ 3. Let the customer talk through his or her anger.

☐ 4. Consider the customer in an objective manner; refuse to take negative comments personally.

☐ 5. Listen with your eyes.

☐ 6. Become distant and less communicative.

☐ 7. Disarm customer by asking: "Are you trying to give me a problem?"

☐ 8. Start to whistle.

☐ 9. Send back the kind of behavior you are receiving.

☐ 10. Immediately steel yourself with a pleasant smile and say to yourself: "I'll show everyone I can handle this customer in such a way she will want to return to us for service in the future."

Acceptable responses: 3, 4, 5, and 10

SIX UNFORGIVABLE MISTAKES

(Check those you intend to avoid.)

☐ Failure to carefully plan each selling day ahead of time.

☐ Waiting for someone else to motivate you.

☐ Failure to develop a strategy which will cover all four bases with qualified prospects.

☐ Giving up too soon on a qualified prospect.

☐ Refusing to take advantage of an opportunity to close the sale.

☐ Failure to maintain good relations with key customers before you lose them.

A BUSINESS CAN'T AFFORD TO LOSE A SINGLE CUSTOMER

SELLING AND
TIME MANAGEMENT

As a salesperson you will have considerable freedom. How you control this freedom is up to you. Failure to manage your time is an easy way to end a selling career.

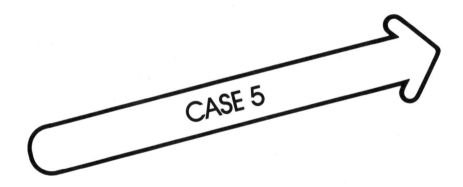

CASE 5

WHO WILL WIN THE TRIP TO HAWAII?

Susan and Eddie occupy identical sales positions with the same firm. A contest is underway; and because of their excellent sales records, both Susan and Eddie are in a good position to win first prize: a trip to Hawaii. The contest will end in three months.

Susan and Eddie are outstanding in using professional selling techniques. Both cover all four bases with ease. But Susan is unbeatable when it comes to personality, initial contacts, and getting customers to like her. Susan feeds on her own success, and her enthusiasm is catching. There is one problem, however. Susan has a tendency to burn out after a few weeks. Somehow, after a highly successful selling period, she falls apart for awhile. Some of this may be because she wears herself out physically, but most of it occurs because she doesn't plan ahead and organize her time on a daily, sustainable basis. Susan works more on impulse than strategy; enthusiasm than logic. When she is in tune, she is fantastic; but when Susan has down-periods, it takes her time to climb back.

Eddie is the opposite. Although he does not enjoy peak selling periods like Susan, Eddie is always in charge of himself. He plans every day ahead of time and sets priorities methodically. Eddie makes the best possible use of his time because he always knows what he is going to do next. He is known among his co-workers as "Steady Eddie" and is highly respected as a professional salesperson. Eddie is measurably better at keeping old customers happy than Susan.

Will Susan win the trip to Hawaii or will Eddie?

Which individual do you feel has the best chance?

☐ I vote for Susan. ☐ I vote for Eddie.

Compare your selection with that of the author on page 54.

MOST PEOPLE GIVE UP SELLING CAREERS BECAUSE
THEY BECOME DISCOURAGED–NOT BECAUSE THEY
LACK THE SKILLS TO SUCCEED.

THE FORMULA ON THE NEXT PAGE WILL ACT AS A
REMINDER TO HELP YOU SUCCEED DURING THE DAYS
AHEAD. YOU MAY WISH TO ATTACH IT TO YOUR
REFRIGERATOR OR BATHROOM MIRROR.

SALES SUCCESS FORMULA

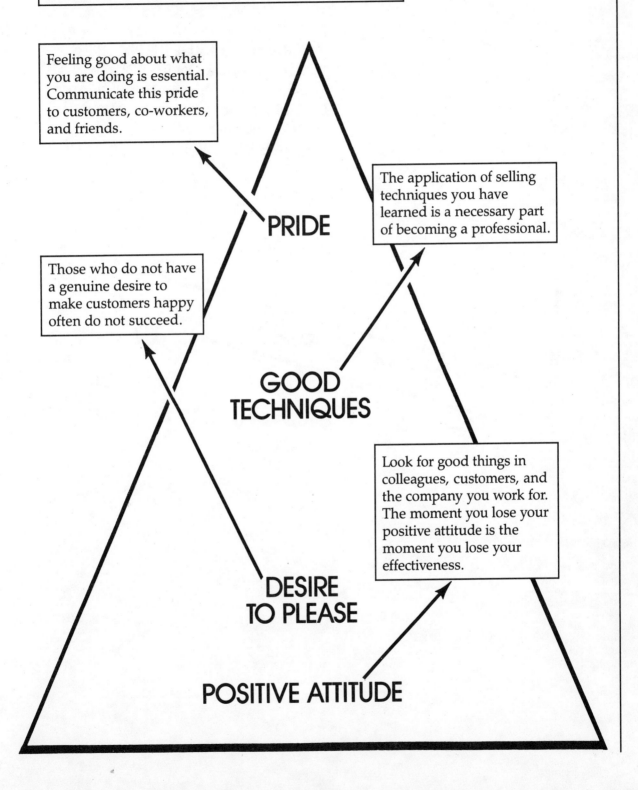

Feeling good about what you are doing is essential. Communicate this pride to customers, co-workers, and friends.

The application of selling techniques you have learned is a necessary part of becoming a professional.

Those who do not have a genuine desire to make customers happy often do not succeed.

Look for good things in colleagues, customers, and the company you work for. The moment you lose your positive attitude is the moment you lose your effectiveness.

PRIDE

GOOD TECHNIQUES

DESIRE TO PLEASE

POSITIVE ATTITUDE

IT IS TIME TO MEASURE THE PROGRESS YOU HAVE MADE. ON THE FOLLOWING PAGE ARE 20 STATEMENTS WHICH ARE EITHER TRUE OR FALSE. EACH IS WORTH 5 POINTS. ANSWERS WILL BE FOUND ON THE PAGE FOLLOWING THE TEST.

SCORE YOURSELF

DEMONSTRATE YOUR PROGRESS

For each statement below, put a check under true or false.

True *False*

____ ____ 1. Financial institutions do not need to teach their people selling techniques.

____ ____ 2. There are more successes than failures in selling.

____ ____ 3. Without a positive attitude, good sales techniques are useless.

____ ____ 4. Quiet people, even those with great confidence, are seldom successful at selling.

____ ____ 5. Salespeople who view themselves as consultants have a psychological edge over others.

____ ____ 6. Comparing selling to baseball emphasizes the point that selling is a process rather than a single event.

____ ____ 7. The best place to discover a prospect's needs is toward the end of the sales pitch.

____ ____ 8. Most customers are more interested in facts than benefits.

____ ____ 9. The best way to keep a customer happy is to practice the Mutual Reward Theory.

____ ____ 10. A professional salesperson should never ask for an order.

____ ____ 11. Grooming plays a minor role in communicating a good image.

____ ____ 12. A skillfull salesperson always attempts to make customers feel better about themselves.

____ ____ 13. When customers raise objections, it usually means they have begun to make up their minds.

____ ____ 14. Related selling is when you suggest other items that complement each other.

____ ____ 15. Professional salespeople rely on in-person calls and disdain the use of the telephone.

____ ____ 16. It is more difficult to keep an old customer than find a new one.

____ ____ 17. Learning selling techniques in a retail store can improve one's career in all areas.

____ ____ 18. The way to become a professional salesperson is to analyze mistakes and then make behavioral changes so you don't repeat the same mistake.

____ ____ 19. Closing the sale is the easiest part of selling.

____ ____ 20. A positive attitude plus good sales techniques constitutes the best possible formula for selling success.

TOTAL   Turn page for answers.

ANSWERS TO EXERCISE OF PAGE 51:

1. F More and more banks are teaching selling techniques.
2. F Countless people have tried selling and turned to other careers.
3. T A negative attitude will turn a customer away even if the salesperson uses good techniques.
4. F Quiet, sensitive salespeople can be extremely successful.
5. T This is true because they listen better and are more in tune with the problem of the customer.
6. T All steps are important, but it is the way the process is put together that makes the difference.
7. F Third base is too late in the process; first base is the right answer.
8. F Although customers appreciate some facts, they are more interested in what the product or service will do for them.
9. T When both the customer and the salesperson come out ahead (the purpose of the Mutual Reward Theory), the relationship continues.
10. F Asking for the order at the right time is highly professional.
11. F Grooming plays a major role because sometimes a salesperson does not get a second chance to make a good impression.
12. T If you make someone feel better about him or herself you have strengthened your relationship with that person.
13. T That is why all objections should be encouraged.
14. T Suggesting additional products is the sign of a good salesperson.
15. F Professional salespeople make maximum use of the telephone to save time and money.
16. T This is especially true if the customer has been neglected.
17. T Successful executives often start out as salespeople.
18. T Self-analysis is critical after each selling experience.
19. F The most difficult part of the selling process is the close.
20. T The combination of a positive attitude and good techniques is unbeatable if the welfare of the customer is realized.

LOOKING AHEAD

CONGRATULATIONS! Your score indicates the progress you have made in a short period of time.

How can you become increasingly successful?
Here are 5 tips.

1. Review this material often.

2. Apply several of the concepts in this book immediately as you work.

3. Discuss your selling experiences with your manager to better evaluate your progress by using the Voluntary Contract on page v.

4. Order and read other self-help books listed on page 55 such as *Personal Time Management, Attitude: Your Most Priceless Possession, Successful Self-Management* and *Quality Customer Service*.

5. Practice, practice, practice!

AUTHOR'S SUGGESTED ANSWERS

A Decision For Ramona. Sales training can be a great confidence builder and personality ''booster''. Should Ramona take advantage of the sales training and become a professional, she will enhance her future in all directions.

Will Joe Survive? It is the opinion of the author that Joe will fail unless he learns to take selling seriously. Personality alone is not enough. In fact, soft-spoken, well-organized salespeople, who are good listeners, usually outsell those who rely excessively on their personality. Joe seems to feel selling is a piece of cake. Until he accepts it as a profession requiring self-discipline, his chances of survival are poor.

Who Made The Sale? Although it could go either way, the author would give the edge to Mary because of her deeper product knowledge and the fact that committee members seemed more involved in her presentation. The more one knows about a product, the more confidence that person has in selling it. This probably came through more during Mary's presentation than in Sally's. In spending other people's money, the committee members would probably lean toward the salesperson who stressed long-wear qualities and could back that claim up with facts.

Who Closed The Sale? All other things being equal, the author believes Marlow stands the better chance of closing the sale. Reasons: (1) The problem-solving approach is usually more effective. (2) Building up to a climax, if not overdone, can swing a normal prospect in your direction. (3) Marlow's closing sentence is more powerful and stands a chance of getting an immediate ''yes.'' Sara's closing sentence gives the prospect an opportunity to retreat. For those who may feel Marlow's close contained too much pressure, the reader is reminded that getting to third base was a big investment in time and effort. Providing the bases were covered well, a strong close would be in order.

Who Will Win The Trip To Hawaii? It will be a close race, but the author votes for Eddie because organization usually pays off in the long run. Susan will have trouble maintaining her enthusiasm over a three-month period while Eddie will probably show greater consistency. If Susan eliminated her down-periods, she could be a runaway winner.

THE FIFTY-MINUTE SERIES

Quantity	Title	Code #	Price	Amount
	The Fifty-Minute Supervisor—*2nd Edition*	58-0	$6.95	
	Effective Performance Appraisals—*Revised*	11-4	$6.95	
	Successful Negotiation—*Revised*	09-2	$6.95	
	Quality Interviewing—*Revised*	13-0	$6.95	
	Team Building: An Exercise in Leadership—*Revised*	16-5	$7.95	
	Performance Contracts: The Key To Job Success—*Revised*	12-2	$6.95	
	Personal Time Management	22-X	$6.95	
	Effective Presentation Skills	24-6	$6.95	
	Better Business Writing	25-4	$6.95	
	Quality Customer Service	17-3	$6.95	
	Telephone Courtesy & Customer Service	18-1	$6.95	
	Restaurant Server's Guide To Quality Service—*Revised*	08-4	$6.95	
	Sales Training Basics—*Revised*	02-5	$6.95	
	Personal Counseling—*Revised*	14-9	$6.95	
	Balancing Home & Career	10-6	$6.95	
	Mental Fitness: A Guide To Emotional Health	15-7	$6.95	
	Attitude: Your Most Priceless Possession	21-1	$6.95	
	Preventing Job Burnout	23-8	$6.95	
	Successful Self-Management	26-2	$6.95	
	Personal Financial Fitness	20-3	$7.95	
	Job Performance and Chemical Dependency	27-0	$7.95	
	Career Discovery—*Revised*	07-6	$6.95	
	Study Skills Strategies—*Revised*	05-X	$6.95	
	I Got The Job!—*Revised*	59-9	$6.95	
	Effective Meetings Skills	33-5	$7.95	
	The Business of Listening	34-3	$6.95	
	Professional Sales Training	42-4	$7.95	
	Customer Satisfaction: The Other Half of Your Job	57-2	$7.95	
	Managing Disagreement Constructively	41-6	$7.95	
	Professional Excellence for Secretaries	52-1	$6.95	
	Starting A Small Business: A Resource Guide	44-0	$7.95	
	Developing Positive Assertiveness	38-6	$6.95	
	Writing Fitness-Practical Exercises for Better Business Writing	35-1	$7.95	
	An Honest Day's Work: Motivating Employees to Give Their Best	39-4	$6.95	
	Marketing Your Consulting & Professional Services	40-8	$7.95	
	Time Management On The Telephone	53-X	$6.95	
	Training Managers to Train	43-2	$7.95	
	New Employee Orientation	46-7	$6.95	
	The Art of Communicating: Achieving Impact in Business	45-9	$7.95	
	Technical Presentation Skills	55-6	$7.95	
	Plan B: Protecting Your Career from the Winds of Change	48-3	$7.95	
	A Guide To Affirmative Action	54-8	$7.95	
	Memory Skills in Business	56-4	$6.95	

(Continued on next page)

THE FIFTY-MINUTE SERIES
(Continued)

☐ Send volume discount information.

☐ Add my name to CPI's mailing list.

	Amount
Total (from other side)	
Shipping ($1.50 first book, $.50 per title thereafter)	
California Residents add 7% tax	
Total	

Ship to: _____

_____

_____

_____

Phone number: _____

Bill to: _____

_____

_____

_____

P.O. # _____

**All orders except those with a P.O.# must be prepaid.
Call (415) 949-4888 for more information.**

BUSINESS REPLY

FIRST CLASS   PERMIT NO. 884   LOS ALTOS, CA

POSTAGE WILL BE PAID BY ADDRESSEE

NO POSTAGE
NECESSARY
IF MAILED
IN THE
UNITED STATES

Crisp Publications, Inc.
95 First Street
Los Altos, CA 94022